W9-CKI-163

LET'S CELEBRATE AMERICA

THE STATUE OF LIBERTY
A Welcome Gift

by Joanne Mattern

RED
CHAIR
·PRESS·

Let's Celebrate America is produced and published by Red Chair Press:

Red Chair Press LLC   PO Box 333   South Egremont, MA 01258-0333

www.redchairpress.com

About the Author

Joanne Mattern is a former editor and the author of nearly 350 books for children and teens. She began writing when she was a little girl and just never stopped! Joanne loves nonfiction because she enjoys bringing history and science topics to life and showing young readers that nonfiction is full of compelling stories! Joanne lives in New York State with her husband, four children, and several pets.

Publisher's Cataloging-In-Publication Data

Names: Mattern, Joanne, 1963–

Title: The Statue of Liberty : a welcome gift / by Joanne Mattern.

Description: South Egremont, MA : Red Chair Press, [2017] | Series: Let's celebrate America | Interest age level: 008-012. | Includes a glossary and references for additional reading. | "Core content classroom."--Cover. | Includes bibliographical references and index. | Summary: "She was a gift of friendship and peace between France and the United States. 'Liberty Enlightening the World' stands now as a symbol of America's embrace of freedom and democracy. Find out why 4 million visitors each year come to see this majestic statue in New York's harbor."--Provided by publisher.

Identifiers: LCCN 2016954996 | ISBN 978-1-63440-224-8 (librar   y hardcover) | ISBN 978-1-63440-234-7 (paperback) | ISBN 978-1-63440-244-6 (ebook)

Subjects: LCSH: Statue of Liberty (New York, N.Y.)--Juvenile literature. | Signs and symbols--United States--Juvenile literature. | CYAC: Statue of Liberty (New York, N.Y.) | Signs and symbols--United States.

Classification: LCC F128.64.L6 M38 2017 (print) | LCC F128.64.L6 (ebook) | DDC 974.7/1--dc23

Photo credits: p. 7, 10, 18: Granger; 4, 6, 8, 12, 14, 15, 17, 21, 22, 25, 29, 31: Library of Congress; 26, 28, 30: National Park Service; cover, p. 1, 3, 8, 9, 11, 19, 23, 24, 25, 27, 32, back cover: Shutterstock

Printed in the United States of America

0517 1P WRZF17

Table of Contents

The Lady with the Lamp

The shouts heard below deck came in Polish, Italian, and Yiddish. But they all had the same message: "There she is!" After weeks at sea, Anton knew what this meant. It was the shout he had been waiting for since he and his parents left his friends and relatives in Poland. He rushed up on deck to join a growing crowd of passengers gazing out over New York City's harbor. Pushing his way to the railing, he could finally see her: The Statue of **Liberty**.

Suddenly, Anton noticed the crowd around him. Like Anton, everyone was filled with emotion. Some cheered, others wept. One woman bowed her head in prayer. Before heading back through the crowd, he turned and gazed once more into the face of Lady Liberty. For the first time he truly understood why his parents had brought him here, to America.

During the late 1800s and early 1900s, millions of **immigrants** arrived in New York Harbor after a long journey on board overcrowded ships. These immigrants left their homelands in search of a new life in the United States. Many of them left places threatened by war, famine, and poverty. They all had a dream that better things were waiting for them in their new home.

When these immigrants sailed toward the city of New York, they saw an amazing sight. A giant statue of a woman holding up a torch greeted them in the harbor. The woman seemed to be calling them forward, lighting their way to a better life.

In truth, the Statue of Liberty, as she was called, had nothing to do with immigration. Instead, the statue was a gift of friendship between two nations. However, over the years, this statue became a symbol of freedom and hope to people all over the world.

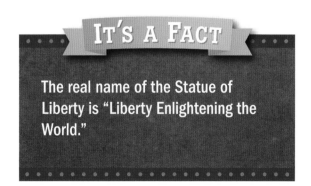

IT'S A FACT

The real name of the Statue of Liberty is "Liberty Enlightening the World."

Friends in France

Edouard de Laboulaye

The story of the Statue of Liberty began in France in 1865. One night, a French professor named Edouard de Laboulaye [duh Lah-boo-lie] gave a dinner party for some of his friends. Years earlier, France had supported the United States when the new nation fought for its independence from Great Britain. Soon after the American Revolution ended, the French Revolution began. Between 1789–1799, French citizens fought to get rid of the **monarchy** and create a more **democratic** government. Citizens demanded "liberty, equality, and fraternity." Although the French Revolution did achieve some of its goals, it did not win them the independence that the Americans had.

Laboulaye and his friends admired the United States and its democratic government. They felt the two countries had a lot in common. During the party, Laboulaye had a big idea. He told his friend, sculptor Frederic Auguste Bartholdi, that he wanted France to create a **monument** and give it to the United States. The monument would be a gift and also celebrate the idea of liberty that both nations believed in. Bartholdi liked this idea very much.

The mayor of Rouen blocks citizens from entering the Hotel de Ville, or City Hall, during a bread riot in 1793.

The Story of Bartholdi

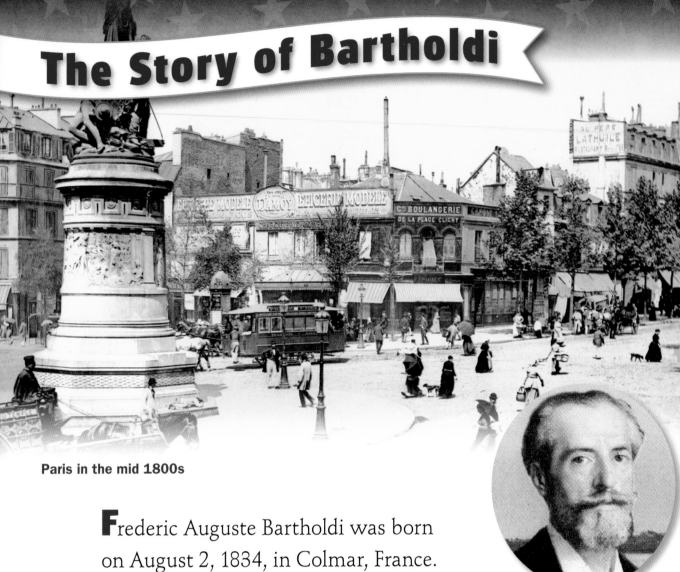

Paris in the mid 1800s

Frederic Auguste Bartholdi

Frederic Auguste Bartholdi was born on August 2, 1834, in Colmar, France. His father died just two years later, and Bartholdi's mother moved the family to Paris.

Bartholdi took lessons in art and sculpture. He was only eighteen years old when he was **commissioned** to create a memorial for a French military hero. People loved the statue he built, and Bartholdi became famous all over France. He went on to create many other works of public art, including statues and fountains.

Bartholdi had big dreams, and he built big sculptures. During a trip to Egypt in 1856, Bartholdi saw the famous pyramids and the statue of the Sphinx. These monuments inspired

Bartholdi to build even bigger. When his friend Laboulaye suggested a larger-than-life statue as a gift to the United States, Bartholdi was ready to take on the project.

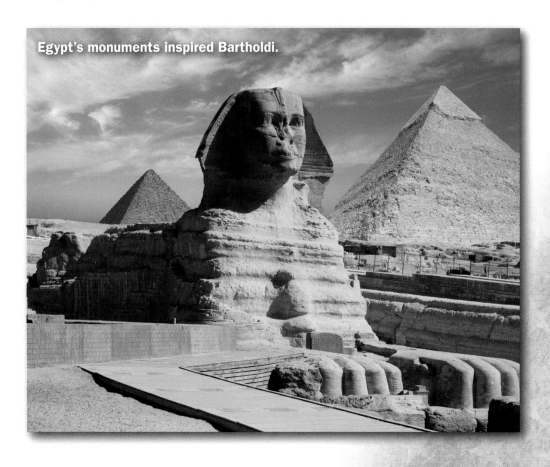

Egypt's monuments inspired Bartholdi.

Looking for Money

In 1871, Bartholdi traveled to the United States. He wanted to find people to pay for and support his idea for a statue. A few months before he arrived, France had overthrown its ruler, Napoleon III, and finally became a **republic**. Because the United States liked the new French government, Bartholdi was sure he could find support for his project.

Bartholdi in his Paris studio.

IT'S A FACT

Bartholdi estimated he needed $250,000 to build his statue.

Bartholdi met with politicians and businessmen all over the United States. Many people supported his idea. Back in France, many French people also wanted to see the statue built. Some of them formed a group called the Union Franco-Americaine to raise money for the project. Many **donations** also came from children and ordinary citizens.

In 1875, Bartholdi displayed a small plaster model of his statue at a fund-raising dinner held by the Union Franco-Americaine. After that, many wealthy French families and American businesses donated money. At last, Bartholdi could get to work.

A Classic Figure

In the 19th century, many important monuments used the classic female figure to stand for an important ideal such as freedom or democracy. So Bartholdi's Lady Liberty was not unusual for his day. In fact, the statue uses many classic symbols inspired by ancient Rome and Greece: the long Roman robe, the simple sandals, the glowing torch, the ancient tablet, and the spiked crown. Bartholdi carefully designed his statue to reflect American ideals of democracy, opportunity, hope and freedom.

The seven spikes on the crown of the statue represent the seven seas and continents of the world.

A Statue Takes Shape

Bartholdi began working in his studio in Paris. He knew he faced many challenges. He wrote that the statue had to be "light, easily worked, of good appearance and yet strong enough to stand the stress of a long ocean voyage–and must be almost impervious to the effect of the salt-laden air of New York Harbor."

Workmen constructing the Statue of Liberty in Bartholdi's Parisian workshop.

Bartholdi knew he could not complete his work all by himself. He met with an engineer named Alexandre Gustave Eiffel. A few years later, Eiffel would design Paris' famous Eiffel Tower. Eiffel came up with the idea of having a huge iron rod in the center of the statue. The outer layers of the statue would be made of thin sheets of copper. These sheets would be attached to the center framework by another set of iron bars.

Eiffel's plan was a good one. Bartholdi built a four-foot-tall plaster model of the statue. This model was a guide to the carpenters and coppersmiths who worked on the statue.

Bartholdi wanted his noble statue to be active, reflecting the great struggle that Americans endured for their freedom. To do this, he depicted the statue as if she is striding forward, with one foot in front of the other. Broken chains lay at her feet, symbolizing Liberty's escape from the chains of tyranny.

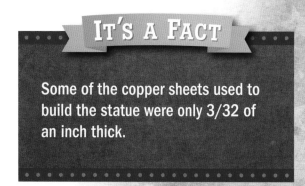

IT'S A FACT

Some of the copper sheets used to build the statue were only 3/32 of an inch thick.

A Trip to America

In 1876, the United States celebrated its 100th birthday. The statue was nowhere near ready by that date, but Bartholdi did find a way to add his creation to America's celebrations. In August 1876, the statue's arm and torch were taken apart and shipped to Philadelphia, where the United States was holding a Centennial Exposition. Once the sculpture arrived, it was put back together and put on display.

Hand and torch on display in Philadelphia at the Centennial Exposition in 1876.

An exhibit hall showing American machinery at the Centennial Exposition

Everyone at the Exhibition loved the sculpture. Visitors eagerly walked inside the arm and climbed a ladder up to the torch. After the Centennial Exposition closed, the sculpture was displayed in New York City. Once again, visitors were happy to pay a small fee of fifty cents to climb inside.

Bartholdi was also in the United States at this time. He spent eight months traveling around the country to raise money for the statue. In January, 1877, a committee formed to raise money for the statue's **pedestal**. Then, in February, 1877, Congress authorized the United States to accept the statue and provide a site for it. Bedloe's Island in New York Harbor would be the statue's new home, just as Bartholdi wanted.

The Statue Grows Bigger

As soon as Bartholdi returned to France, he started work on the statue's head. In 1878, the head was exhibited at the Paris International Exposition. Crowds lined the streets to watch the head travel to the Exposition. Just as people had done in America when the arm was displayed, thousands of visitors came to climb into the head and look out the windows at the top.

By December of 1882, the statue was too big to be kept inside Bartholdi's workshop. He wrote, "The statue commences to reach above the houses, and next spring you will see it overlook the entire city."

A newspaper reporter was amazed at the size of the statue. He wrote, "The whole scene abounded in this curiosity of measurement… Her lips, from dimple to dimple, were as long as my walking stick, and fifteen people, I was told, might sit around the flame of her torch."

Finally, in March 1885, the statue was finished and ready to ship to the United States. There was just one problem. The United States was not ready.

MONUMENT de l'INDEPENDANCE

A Plea for the Pedestal

Excitement at the arrival in New York from France of the ship carrying Frederic Bartholdi's Statue of Liberty. In the foreground is the unfinished pedestal.

In 1885, the statue was broken down into 350 pieces for its journey to the U.S. It took 241 crates to carry the precious cargo aboard the French ship *Isere*. The ship arrived in America to great fanfare. But the funds had run out and the pedestal was still not complete. It was an embarrassment to both countries—it seemed the Americans did not want the precious gift from France.

Fortunately, the Statue of Liberty had a powerful champion. A Hungarian immigrant named Joseph Pulitzer had come to America as a young boy in 1864. In less than 20 years, he owned several newspapers, including a New York daily called *The World*. He decided to use his newspaper to encourage people to contribute to the pedestal. Pulitzer was especially angry that wealthy people had not been much help. He offered to accept any donation, no matter how small.

Money poured in. Most of it was donated by poor people and children. Over 120,000 people donated. On August 11, 1885, less than six months after starting his campaign, Pulitzer announced that $100,000 had been raised.

IT'S A FACT

It is believed that Bartholdi modeled the face of the statue after his own mother.

A Beacon of Hope

The Statue of Liberty quickly became a popular tourist attraction. Thousands of people climbed narrow, winding staircases inside the statue. They looked out of windows in the torch and the crown.

The statue became even more important to the immigrants who flooded into the United States over the next thirty years. The statue was one of the first things immigrants saw when they arrived in New York. The gleaming torch seemed to call them like a light promising hope and a better life.

In 1883, Emma Lazarus wrote a poem called "The New Colossus." Over time, the poem became linked to the Statue of Liberty and her promise to new Americans. In 1903, the poem was engraved on a tablet and placed inside the base of the statue.

**"Keep, ancient lands, your storied pomp!" cries she
With silent lips. "Give me your tired, your poor,
Your huddled masses yearning to breathe free, …"**

–From 'The New Colossus' by Emma Lazarus

IT'S A FACT

The Statue of Liberty has some amazing measurements! Here are just a few:

Height of statue: 151 feet, 1 inch

Length of index finger: 8 feet, 1 inch

Width of head (ear to ear): 10 feet

Length of nose: 4 feet, 6 inches

Length of right arm: 42 feet

Height of pedestal: 89 feet

Weight of statue: 450,000 pounds

The National Park Service Takes Over

Several things changed at the statue over the years. The War Department was in charge of the statue between 1901 and 1933. They built army barracks and a radio station on the island. In 1924, the statue was declared a national monument. Nine years later, the National Park Service took responsibility for taking care of the statue.

The Ellis Island National Monument is part of the Statue of Liberty National Park. The Main Building on Ellis Island is now a museum dedicated to the history of immigration.

The statue had many physical problems. The arm became unsafe for visitors and was closed in 1916. Rainwater leaked in through the copper plates and rusted the inside of the statue. The pedestal also needed repairs. The statue was closed during the late 1930s to fix these problems.

The National Park Service set up many **exhibits** at the Statue of Liberty. These exhibits emphasized the statue's role as a beacon of hope to the world. This meaning was especially strong to refugees who fled Europe during and after World War II (1939–1945).

Like a New Penny

When the copper statue was first built, she was actually reddish-brown, like a brand-new penny. The green hue of the statue is caused by a reaction between copper and the many years of rain, wind and ice. Engineers first studied this green film in 1907. They decided it wasn't harming the statue and may actually help protect it.

When the statue was new it was probably closer to the colors above.

The statue's torch was replaced to match the original gold leaf design by Bartholdi.

In 1983, people began to get ready for the Statue of Liberty's 100th birthday. Organizations formed to raise money. The statue was closed and repaired once again. French and American workers replaced the rusted inner framework and created a new flame. They also installed an elevator so visitors would no longer have to climb the narrow staircases.

The new flame in place

In 1984, the Statue of Liberty was named a UNESCO World Heritage Site. UNESCO described the statue as a "masterpiece of the human spirit" and a powerful symbol of liberty, peace, human rights, democracy, and opportunity.

On the Fourth of July, 1986, the statue reopened with a big celebration. A parade of ships sailed through the harbor. That night, fireworks lit the sky. President Ronald Reagan spoke at the event, saying, "We are the keepers of the flame of liberty; we hold it high for the world to see." Millions of people watched the event, both in the harbor and on television. It was a grand celebration!

Index